WIS-AND DOM LIFE

EX· LIBRIS

DONALD R. WALDOCH

THE JAPANESE HOUSE

Its Interior and Exterior

THE JAPANESE HOUSE
Its Interior and Exterior

by Tatsuo and Kiyoko Ishimoto

BONANZA BOOKS · NEW YORK

Books by Tatsuo Ishimoto

THE ART OF FLOWER ARRANGEMENT

THE ART OF THE JAPANESE GARDEN

THE ART OF GROWING MINIATURE TREES, PLANTS AND LANDSCAPES

THE ART OF DRIFTWOOD AND DRIED ARRANGEMENTS

THE ART OF PLANT AND DRIFTWOOD ARRANGEMENT

A TREASURY OF JAPANESE FLOWER ARRANGEMENTS

A TREASURY OF DRIFTWOOD ARRANGEMENTS

CONTENTS

INTRODUCTION

In the last decade or so America has been "discovering" Japan. One Japanese idea after another has crossed the Pacific to add variety and freshness to our daily living. Americans already know and appreciate Japanese flower arrangement, Japanese garden design, and bonsai, the art of growing miniature trees in containers. In the nineteen-fifties I published books on each of these subjects and all proved popular.*

Imports from Japan increase in quantity and variety each year. Now coming to us are such traditional things as folk pottery, such modern, competitive

*The Art of Flower Arrangement, The Art of the Japanese Garden, The Art of Growing Miniature Trees, Plants and Landscapes

items as cameras, binoculars, tape recorders, and portable television sets, and such utilitarian architectural objects as *shoji* and *fusuma* screens, paper and plastic lamp fixtures, *zabuton* pillows, and *tatami* mats.

Japanese architectural ideas caught on first, naturally enough, in the fiftieth state. Hawaiian houses today, whether the householder's name is Nakashima or O'Brien, frequently use both shoji and fusuma screens, even when the floor is standard American oak or tile. In recent years, California architects have also been adopting Japanese architectural ideas and adapting them to American needs. One thing that particularly appeals to Californians is the *engawa* (see page 124), which is used again and again in recently built houses.

Many American magazine editors have visited Japan and, later, expressed their enthusiasm in print. *House Beautiful*'s August 1960 *shibui* issue aroused great interest here. *Sunset,* the popular West Coast magazine, has published numerous articles on how to adapt shoji, engawa, and other Japanese architectural features. And, of course, the Museum of Modern Art in New York City put a complete Japanese house on display in the museum garden as early as 1953.

Today you will see new houses in Japan built with concrete, steel, masonry, stucco, glass. But the classic Japanese house was built basically of wood, with some auxiliary use of paper, tile or thatch, plaster, and stone. Let's consider the traditional Japanese house. It is still being constructed in its classic form, and its design influences even the westernized houses now going up in Japan.

The classic house is framed in wood, posts supporting beams. It is one or two stories, with a gable or hip-and-gable roof covered in tile, thatch, or wood shingles. The foundation consists of large natural stones set into the ground to support the posts. The frame of posts carries the roof load; most of the walls are sliding shoji screens. The interior walls are mostly sliding fusuma screen-partitions.

The floors are thick tatami mats, about three by six feet in size. These mats determine the size of the rooms and the size of the house; they are the module. Because the tatami is soft, you do not wear shoes indoors in a Japanese house.

The garden is part of the Japanese house. It may be postage-stamp size, but it is designed for viewing from indoors, with the shoji rolled back. Often there are several small gardens, to be enjoyed from different rooms.

Even though the Japanese house has always been a handcrafted structure, its design has much in common with that of modern mass-production and prefabricated houses in the United States today. The chief reason is the universal use of a uniform module in Japan, the three- by six-foot tatami mat.

Japanese houses also have much in common with the West's modern and contemporary architecture. Modern houses in America usually make a merit of simplicity—even austerity—in such things as wall surfaces. Natural materials are left natural, redwood or pine stained but not painted. In many instances, rooms in our modern houses have one or more walls of glass looking out on intimate gardens enclosed with simple fencing. Occasionally a glass wall is designed to be rolled back so that you can step directly out of doors. Our present-day houses are often modular too, the most common module being four by eight feet (mass-produced four-by-eight panels are available in America today in everything from gypsum wallboard to plywood, hardboard, insulation board, asbestos-cement board, and other materials). Contemporary houses generally are so built that the structure is revealed—you can see the posts and beams of the house frame in plain view within rooms.

Here, then, are half a dozen distinctive features of many of America's newest houses. What is interesting is that today's Japanese houses also have all of these so-called "modern" characteristics, and they have had them for centuries!

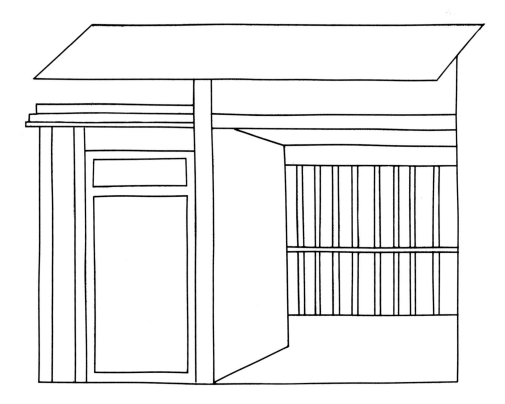

Traditional Japanese country houses near Kyoto. Notice the rice-straw thatch roofs, the privacy hedge, and the modern power pole.

City houses crowd together in Fukuoka. Most roofs are tile. Note the small garden behind the house near the bottom of the photograph.

A look at Japanese houses

Here, to start, are a few pictures of the houses the Japanese build and live in. . . . When you look down from a hill on a Japanese town, at first you see only a tossed sea of roofs, twisting every way (the second photograph above). But after a time you notice additional details: Every roof has its gable. The gables run at right angles to each other, and here and there a tree raises its head. Occasionally you can glimpse other patches of green—crowded as they are, these houses have their bits of private garden.

In the country there is more room, but one characteristic of the city house carries over into rural areas. Even if a sweeping view is at hand, the home-owner may shut it off from the ground floor with a hedge, fence, or wall, to create an intimate and private garden. If his is a two-story house, as a rule the upper floor will take advantage of the view. Even in the country, most

Streetside in a good residential area. Entry gate is roofed, with a fence separating it from the street. The house faces a rear garden.

Streetside in a semibusiness area. The family lives upstairs, above the store at street level. The house next door has an entry garden behind the fence.

houses are inward-turning. They turn their backs on street or road and look inward toward a private and intimate garden.

Roads and streets in Japan have traditionally been of dirt, dusty in the dry season, muddy in the rain. This is changing now; paving is going ahead rapidly in both towns and rural neighborhoods. But dust and mud are sometimes still a problem, as once they always were, and they have had an influence on Japanese house design.

At the entry you will usually cross a bit of paving or an area of loose stones. The homeowner frequently wets this area down, to lay the dust and to create a clean, fresh transition between road and house.

Mud and dust are also one reason why the floor level of the Japanese house is raised and one reason it has become the custom to remove outdoor footwear as you enter.

Country: The narrow dirt road passes a rice field. In the distance is a cluster of country houses.

Country village: The road is dirt. Walkers keep to the left. Oncoming bicycle also is "driving left," as in England.

In today's Japan

A serious look at the Japanese house must begin with a look at the Japanese people. Their way of life is different from ours. Most Japanese still dress differently from Westerners, although more and more are wearing Western-style clothing at least part of the time.

The Japanese sit differently (and without chairs at home), sleep differently (without what we would call a bed), eat differently (with chopsticks), and eat different foods (including raw fish and dried seaweed). And all of these differences have affected the design of the Japanese house.

Consider the street scenes here. These are the people who go home to the Japanese house. Turn the page to meet more of today's Japanese away from home—most of them at work, but two playing a game!

City: This Nagoya sidewalk is paved but the street still is gravel. Notice the variety in street dress.

Shopping: This couple wear the traditional Japanese summer costume. Men everywhere in Japan walk in geta like these.

Sidewalk fruit stand: Note the pay telephone; also the mixture of Western and Japanese dress.

Sidewalk in Tokyo: Notice the hanging paper lanterns, the gay signs, and here again, the variety of dress.

The riverman

The farmer

The landscapers

Here are a few of today's Japanese, busy outdoors and indoors

Here are some twenty Japanese at work and two at play. Notice how they sit (or kneel). Most Westerners find it very uncomfortable to assume these positions, but the Japanese have used them since childhood. Note, too, the height and nature of the benches and tables. And how many people are using their hands. The hands—almost by themselves—are the tools with which this traditionally handicraft nation has accomplished its work.

At home, these people live in much the same manner as at work. They use very little furniture; they sit (in reasonable comfort, on zabuton) directly on the floor. Cooking at home is a handicraft procedure (including the cutting up of the vegetables and meat, and the *designing* of the meal itself). Flower-arranging is an art-handicraft practiced constantly. The serving of tea can be a tradition-shaped ceremony too elaborate to discuss here, but again a *personal*, handcrafted performance.

So perhaps it is only natural that such a handicraft people should live in handcrafted houses.

The silkwashers

The fence-maker

The salesgirl

The salesman

The geta-maker

The seafood-sorter

The retoucher

The flower-arranger

The brush-painter

The fan-maker

The ceramic-painter

Shogi-players

Now, let's visit some Japanese houses

In the half-generation since World War II ended, Japan has experienced extraordinary changes. Many of the changes you can sum up under the broad term westernization. As we have seen on the preceding pages, people are rapidly adopting Western dress—more men are wearing suits and leather shoes, fewer women are appearing in kimono and geta. Among the higher-income families today, an increasing number own cars, own and watch television, and own and use miniature cameras.

Japanese houses also are changing. Many new houses include one or more Western-style rooms, or sometimes a complete floor arranged and furnished much as our houses are furnished. But rarely is the whole house done in Western style. The traditional Japanese house makes sense to the Japanese, and this book will show you why.

All Japanese houses have certain things in common—among them, the use of tatami, shoji, and fusuma; the relationship of entry to street; the entry gate; the manner of entry into the house. On the pages that follow we will introduce you first to these common elements. Together they make up a *vocabulary* of the Japanese house.

But first, here is a 14-page
picture and text presentation
of the *vocabulary* of the Japanese house. . . .

The entry gate leads first to a garden, then to the house

Although a small Japanese house close to a city or village street may have its front entrance directly off the street, the traditional detached Japanese house has a wall, fence, or hedge on the property line around the garden, with a gate to dramatize the entrance. The gate will open to a garden pathway that leads to the entry. Most often, the small entry garden will be separate from the main garden, planned to be enjoyed from the main rooms, usually at the sides and rear of the house.

This photograph shows such a gate. Notice that it is roofed over and has two separate openings. The smaller gate, open here, is for the everyday use of family and servants. The larger gate is opened for guests and on ceremonial occasions. Sometimes there will be a single broad gate, with a smaller opening in one of the doors for everyday use.

At the *genkan* (entry vestibule) you take off your shoes

The path from the gate leads you to a sheltered enclosure like this one. Its chief elements are a broad step, a platform, then the floor of the house itself.

The stone step is called *kutsunugi-ishi,* or taking-off-shoes stone. You step up and remove your outdoor footwear, be it shoes or geta; you never wear these on the delicate mat-flooring inside a Japanese house.

The intermediate platform-step is called *shikidai,* and is usually of carefully selected and carefully wrought wood. Next to it you will frequently find a cabinet or shelf for depositing your shoes and other gear; here you see an umbrella stand.

The *genkan,* or vestibule, has sliding exterior doors to close it from the outside. It is a small anteroom from which exterior (shoji) panels open to other rooms. Here, the shoji beyond are slid back to reveal a room and a garden on the other side.

The design of the tatami floor of the twelve-mat room beyond repeats that of the foreground room. Notice the occasional absence of the black line of the binding where two mat ends meet.

The floor is resilient *tatami* mats

Laid over a rough subfloor, straw mats cover the entire surface of the floors of the living rooms. These tatami are a little over two inches thick and are composed of a straw core with a surface finish of woven matting. Everywhere they are of the same dimensions: approximately three by six feet. Their side edges are usually bound with a narrow strip of black or dark gray fabric, which is sometimes decorated.

This kind of floor surface contributes many advantages to the Japanese house. One is cleanliness. Since everyone removes his shoes before entering, little or no dirt is tracked in from the outside. The mats may be lifted once or twice a year for a thorough cleaning and airing. Another advantage is quiet. Stockinged or *tabi*-clad feet are quiet in themselves, and on the soft surface of the tatami movement is almost noiseless. A third advantage is comfort. Daily life is carried out sitting or kneeling on the floor, and at night the *futon* (bedding) is laid right on the floor, so the resilience of the mat contributes to such comfort as the Japanese house affords.

The tatami's uniform size has a profound effect on the building of a Japanese house. It is the unit of floor-area measurement. The size of rooms is specified according to the number of mats, and rooms are always laid out so that mats fit precisely, without cutting. Average-sized rooms normally have an even number of mats. The mat's length is repeated in the height of the sliding panels used for interior and exterior walls, and sometimes also its width. Thus, even though the Japanese house is handcrafted, it starts with many of the benefits of modular measure and prefabricated parts.

(Above) *Sliding panels, both of the translucent exterior wall and of the opaque wall at right, are of the same size (three by six) as the mats.*

(Below) *Clean and resilient, tatami present a warm contrast to the outdoors.*

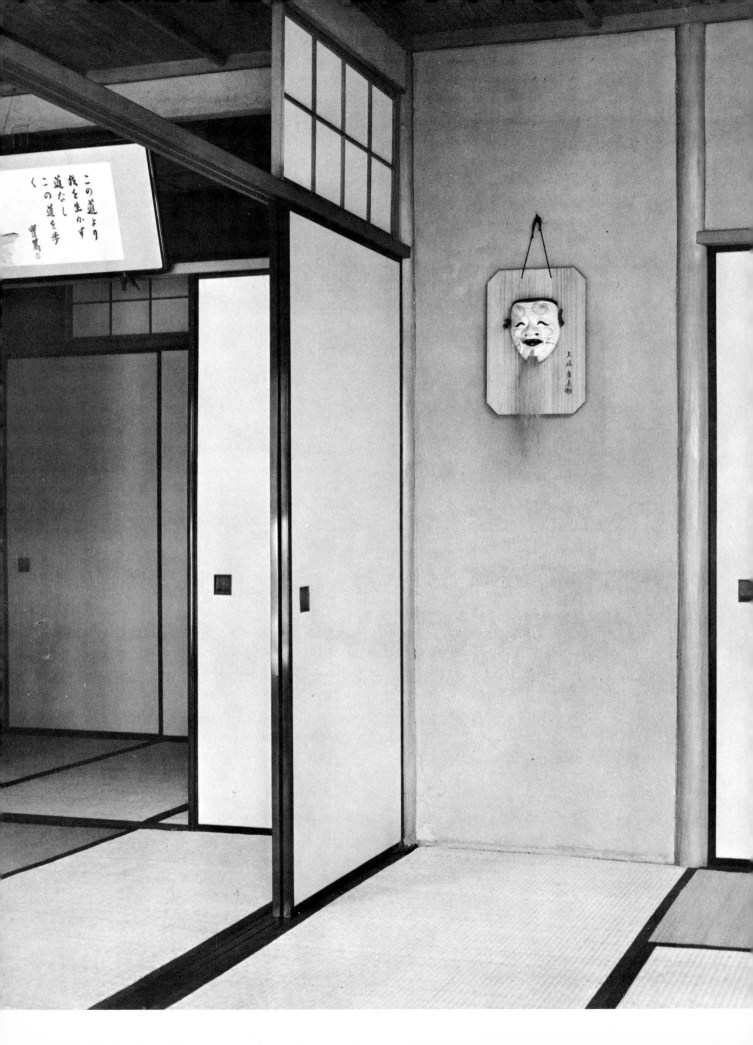

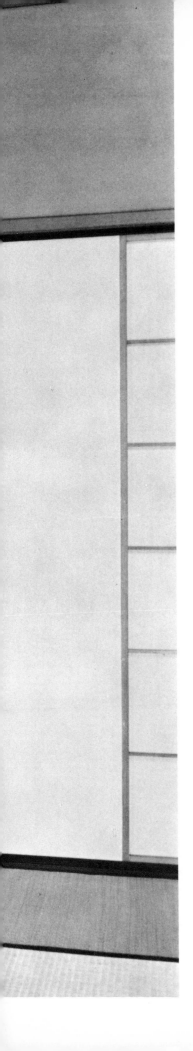

The interior walls
are sliding panels (fusuma)

Although there are some fixed partitions in the Japanese house, most of the interior space is separated—and the rooms defined—by paper-covered fusuma, or sliding interior screens. These rest on a wood surface flush with the top of the tatami, with shallow grooves that serve as tracks to keep them in place. Above them, a lintel—or *kamoi*—six feet high also has tracks on the underside. Between the kamoi and the ceiling there is open space for air circulation when the panels are closed.

By sliding the fusuma back or removing them, the Japanese house achieves large, open interior spaces or combinations of open and closed spaces. In the photograph at the left the fusuma are slid back to open three rooms into one another.

Fusuma may be decorated or plain. Their handles are often richly designed. When used for rooms that will be closed off from an outside wall, they may have a translucent insert, for light. In warm summer weather, solid fusuma may be replaced by open-work panels, often of reed screen, so that air can pass through without a loss of privacy.

The size of fusuma or shoji (see page 28) depends on the width of the room, and is usually the width divided by two or four. Since room size and shape are determined by the tatami module, specifying the number of·mats in a room automatically gives the possible sizes of the sliding panels.

In the *zashiki* (principal room) the focus is on the *tokonoma*

In the Japanese house, the *zashiki* or principal room is a kind of family room used for daily activities, entertaining, eating, and sometimes sleeping. Three of its four walls may be sliding panels, interior and exterior, but the fourth will be devoted to the *tokonoma*.

The tokonoma is an alcove for the display of a scroll, a handsome art object, natural objects such as stones, or a flower arrangement. Seldom are more than two items displayed at one time, and the display is changed seasonally or even more often. The tokonoma is the place of honor in the room—the most honored guest is seated nearest it. A guest room occasionally will have its own tokonoma.

The tokonoma alcove can vary widely in execution, but its basic form is well established. The floor is usually higher than the floor of the room. At one corner is a specially crafted post *(toko-bashira)* often left in its natural state. The ceiling, the same height as that of the room, is obscured by a section of wall in front that acts as a valance. The tokonoma is placed at one end of a rectangular room, usually on the side next to the exterior wall so that it can be lighted by a window in its side.

Adjoining the tokonoma is a smaller recess called the *chigai-dana*. This is generally low-ceilinged, and contains open shelves, a low cabinet, or an upper cabinet. The cabinets are used to store objects for display in the tokonoma. Frequently, as in the picture here, the chigai-dana is also used for a lesser display or arrangement. Sometimes this recess has a window from the tokonoma for light from the side.

The garden room. By moving the shoji, you can radically alter the view from the room.

Exterior wall panels (shoji) slide away

To the Westerner, one of the most charming features of the Japanese house is its translucent sliding exterior wall panels, or shoji. These act both as windows and as doors.

Like fusuma, shoji produce a variety of outlook. You can throw them back partly or completely, to open a room or to open the whole house to the garden. Or they can be completely closed, to bathe the room in a soft, diffused light.

The classic Japanese shoji is made with translucent paper stretched over a wood frame. (On shoji imported to America the covering sometimes is translucent plastic.) Shoji are made in almost endless patterns, but even so are typically quite

The pattern of the shoji is repeated in sliding panels above. Sliding glass doors are beyond.

to reveal the garden

simple in design. In some instances, the lower half is a panel that can be removed, giving still another means of varying the opening. This is a particularly agreeable shoji variation, for it makes it possible to view the garden while you are seated on the floor. In the traditional Japanese house, shoji were protected with rain shutters placed in tracks a small distance out from the house wall.

In the modern Japanese house, shoji are oftentimes combined with other kinds of sliding panels, such as the insect screening shown in the photograph at the left above. They are now also sometimes fitted with glass-panel inserts, or you may see sliding glass doors as well as rain shutters outside.

The *engawa* invites you into the garden

The engawa is many things. It is a narrow platform at the wall line—outside the shoji and inside the rain shutters or sliding glass panels—that extends the indoor floor out over the ground.

The engawa is both step and porch. It provides access from the garden. It is also a place to sit and have tea and cakes on a summer afternoon, much as you would sit on a veranda anywhere. The floor of the engawa is wood; therefore, in many Japanese houses, it is the only place where you can set chairs and a table (you ordinarily do not place such furniture on the tatami floor).

The engawa may be a corridor as well; sometimes it is the only access from room to room when the fusuma inside are closed.

But perhaps the engawa's pleasantest role is as foreground and prelude to the garden, as we see it in these two photographs. It gives depth to the view from any room, beckons you to its edge, and seems to invite you to step down into the garden.

(At left) *Double entry gate as it appears from the street.*

(Left, below) *When the guest gate is open, you can see the front door.*

Inside the gate, the path leads to the front entrance. At left a hedge and screen fence (sodegaki) hide one part of the garden. At right, a tall fence screens another section of garden; you should not presume to pass through this style of gate unless you live here.

From the front gate to the front door

This, the entry to Asaharu Hatada's house, sums up the traditional elements of the approaches to a Japanese house. (The gate is also shown on page 18.)

Note how the garden is closed off from the street. The bamboo property-line fence straddles a rock, part of which shows in the garden on the other side, and circles a tree trunk.

Broad stone steps serve both family and guest side of the gate. In front of them the owner has placed gravel so that dust and mud will not be tracked inside.

Beyond the gate a stone path leads to the sliding front doors. On either side of the path, fencing or planting keeps the garden hidden from the view of callers.

Kutsunugi-ishi: This carefully selected and carefully placed stone step is set in a bed of concrete surfaced with pea gravel. Note the zori (left) and geta.

Getabako: Sliding doors like miniature fusuma make a neat cabinet in the genkan.

Getabako: *The shelves are often simple; sometimes they are left open.*

Getabako: *Shelves hold shoes, zori, and the family's geta, with space for those of callers, plus slippers for inside wear.*

Where to leave your shoes

Since the floor of the Japanese house is well above the ground level, its height is more than you can reach gracefully in one step. The traditional Japanese entry, therefore, has a handsome natural stone or section of log placed on the ground as a first step, an intermediate platform for the removal of shoes, and then a small step to the floor itself.

The stone step (kutsunugi-ishi) is not only an important first impression for the visitor but a real necessity, and so the Japanese take great care in its selection. Its name comes from *kutsu* (shoes), *nugi* (taking off), and *ishi* (stone).

A place to store outdoor footwear (and sometimes to keep slippers for guests) is a usual amenity of the genkan area. Here you see both open and closed shelves. You are less likely to find a full-fledged coat closet, but you may see hooks for hanging coats, a rack for umbrellas (almost a necessity in Japan), and perhaps even a shelf for other parcels—such a shelf was common a century ago for storing the lanterns the Japanese invariably carried at night.

The floor plan is flexible

The typical Japanese house is small. Room size is expressed by the number of mats that cover the floor. A typical size for a living-dining-sleeping room will be six to eight mats (or 108 to 144 square feet), about the size of American bedrooms. Usually, however, this space is not only multipurpose but also readily expandable into other rooms and to the outdoors by means of sliding wall panels.

As shown in the three floor plans below, the entry generally opens into an interior corridor that gives access to most (but not necessarily all) of the living rooms, as well as to the kitchen and bathroom.

Here are three floor plans of Japanese houses. The numbers refer to this glossary list:

1. Entry   *Genkan*
2. Tatami room   *Zashiki*
3. Alcove   *Tokonoma*
4. Closet   *Monoire (Oshiire)*
5. Kitchen   *Daidokoro*
6. Bathroom   *Yokushitsu (Furo)*
7. Porch   *Engawa*

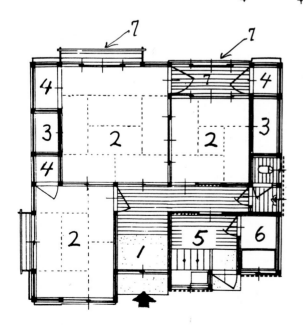

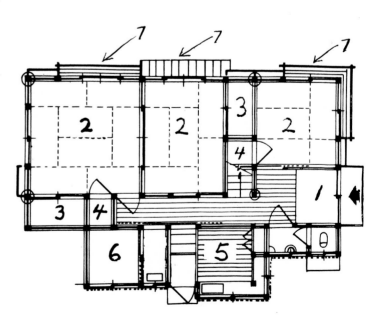

The Japanese room has many functions

The most used and most typical room in the Japanese house is the zashiki, or principal room. It is really a family room. Here the family live and entertain. Here they dine, and here, often, the family (or some members of it) also sleep.

As mentioned before, one of its characteristic features is the tokonoma, where there is always a display of art, a flower arrangement, and perhaps a family treasure or an unusual natural object.

A Japanese living room quickly converts to a sleeping room by the simple process of laying out the bedding on the floor. The bedding is easily put back into the closet in the morning, when the room again assumes one of its many different roles.

This is the zashiki in the home of Kenju Matsushima, designed by Hiroshi Osawa.

The tokonoma takes up part of one end of the zashiki. To the left (out of the picture) is the exterior wall, with shoji; at the right are fusuma. The tokonoma displays a gaku (framed calligraphy panel), a floral arrangement, a pottery figure, and a vase (and the telephone). At the right is a modern version of the chigai-dana.

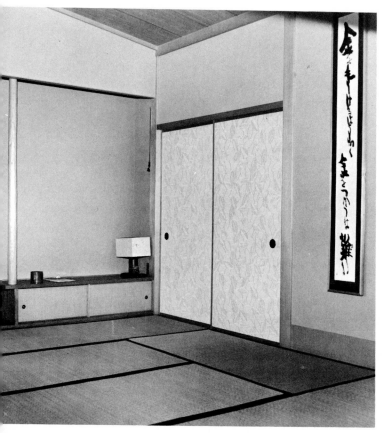

With the closet closed, the panels in this corner of the zashiki look as if they might lead to another room.

With the panels open, you see the closet. Besides clothes, it will usually also contain bedding.

The entry court faces the street. Observe the fence and gate for privacy, the gravel for cleanliness before you step onto the paved court.

The family gate is a sliding section of the larger gate.

For guest use, the entire gate slides to one side.

This modern house simplifies traditional ideas

Here is a fine example of a newly built home with all the needed rooms plus a well-developed garden. It belongs to Michio Matsumoto; the architects were Kodo Matsubara and Tetsuya Ishihara. On these two pages we show you its entry gate and garden. On the next four pages we take a closer look at the house.

Note that although the gate and entry are simplified and somewhat modern-looking, traditional ideas are still there: The gate has two parts. The entry path passes through a garden separate from the main garden onto which the principal rooms open. The seemingly long entry-path suggests a feeling of space sometimes difficult to achieve on a city lot.

You will notice on the floor plan that the living rooms are situated to face the garden, whereas such less-used ones as kitchen, bathroom, and storage rooms are placed at one side.

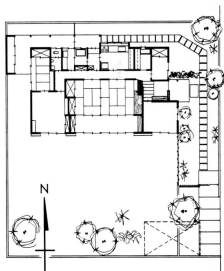

Floor plan. Notice that the house is placed to one side of the lot, making the most of the garden onto which the main rooms face.

Inside the gate, the path leads to the main entry, then around the corner to the rear entry. The light bamboo fence at the left separates entry garden from main garden. The window facing the path has a grille for privacy.

1. *The stone steps and the covered porch are modern and Western. The peeled pole, sliding door, sodegaki, and window grille are all traditional.*

Modern house:
The entry blends the new with the old

Mr. Matsumoto provides unusual comforts for his guests—straw mats to sit on when they take off their shoes, slippers to wear inside the house, and even two blocks of wood to stand on (after removing the shoes) to keep the feet from being chilled by the stone floor (picture at upper right).

Outside the door, note the modern, almost Western, touches: the entry light, the doorbell, the contemporary look of the sodegaki. And yet the whole spirit is still Japanese. Notice how the line of the sodegaki is continued by the hedge to its right.

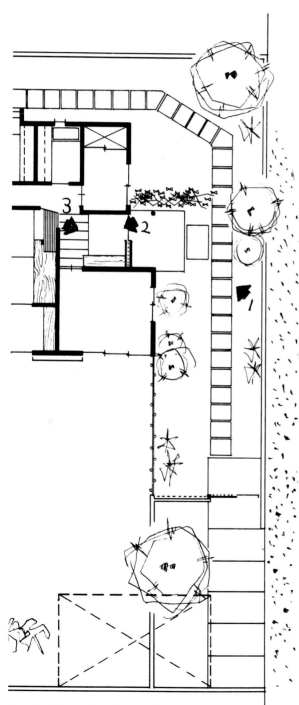

2. *The shikidai and getabako in the vestibule are traditional. Note the mats for sitting.*

3. *The genkan has paving of stone, a shoe cabinet with a modern look, and an umbrella stand.*

On the floor plan above, the numbers show the camera angles of the pictures on these two pages.

1. A simplified version of the tokonoma at one end of the zashiki contains a flower arrangement and a scroll.

Modern house: The parlor and the family room

In the Matsumoto house, the zashiki is kept for receiving guests or for special family occasions, and so functions much as a parlor would. The zashiki is an eight-mat room.

In the adjoining room, which can be opened to or closed from the zashiki by means of fusuma, everyday family activities are carried on. This room has a table set over a recess in the floor (which in cold weather would contain a hibachi for heat). Two floor chairs with backs permit Western-style sitting, with the feet in the sunken area. Two cushions are placed beside the table for Japanese-style sitting. On the shelf are the family television, radio, and record player. Bedding is stored in a closet next to this shelf. The family room is a six-mat room.

2. The adjoining family room opens on the side of the zashiki opposite the tokonoma.

3. At right is the wood-floor hall to which the two rooms open.

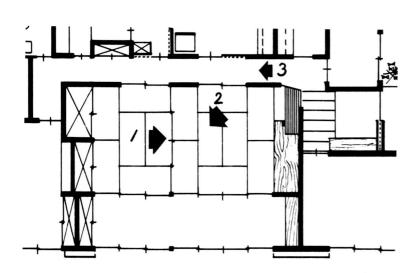

The numbers on the floor plan show where the photos were taken.

The exterior of a multistoried Japanese inn. Note the roof materials: tile, bark, and thatch. The room you see in the other photos is at upper right in this one, beside the large tree.

1. In the Japanese bath, first you wash yourself with water from a small wooden bucket; next you soak in the tub for a while. Then you may get out and wash again, and return to the tub for another soak. The water is usually very hot, and as a rule the effect is therapeutic. Hardier souls often splash cold water on themselves afterward. This sunken tile tub is supplied with hot-springs water (the inn is in Beppu); more commonly, the tub is wooden and the water heated by a wood or gas fire.

The floor plan indicates the camera angles for the numbered photos here and on the next two pages. Shown on the plan are two rooms, and the engawa, closet, bath, and entry.

The Japanese inn: Houses in miniature

Here, in the space of a six-mat and a three-mat room, plus an adjoining bath, are all the functions and most of the parts of a full-scale Japanese house. The maid will bring you a low table for writing or reading, cushions to sit on, bedding to sleep on; she will bring you breakfast, lunch, and dinner. She will see that the tokonoma is properly adorned, and she will open up the shoji to the garden or to the view. Staying in a Japanese inn is an introduction to the life of Japan as well as to the way the Japanese house works.

2. *A corner of the zashiki has a miniature tokonoma; note how simple it can be. The decoration is a calligraphy scroll, flowers, and a Japanese doll in a glass case.*

3. *The air cooler in the wall opposite the tokonoma is a modern innovation. Note the decorated chest and decorated fusuma.*

4. *The zashiki becomes a bedroom when the futon is brought out from the closet and spread on the floor. Beside the pillow is a small floor-lamp.*

5. *Here is a corner of the zashiki, with the shoji closed. The horizontal panels on the left side can be opened either top or bottom (or both). When you are seated on the floor, it is pleasant to have an opening at floor level.*

The Japanese inn: Magic with sliding panels

After centuries of experience, the Japanese have refined the technique of living in a small space. The secret is multiple: they use sliding panels, which do not take up usable floor space as hinged doors do, and which offer a variety of openings and closures; they also use portable appointments (bedding, cushions for seating, low tables) that can be compactly stowed away when not in use.

Here, in a Japanese inn, is a demonstration of some of this versatility. The combinations of openings possible with the shoji at left, offer a variety of visual experience (and of ventilation). The storage combinations at the right take care of all dressing and sleeping needs. The main room is 9 x 12 feet; the anteroom is 6 x 9 feet.

The same corner with the shoji open. Those on the right have panels that slide up within each frame, and the entire panel will also slide to the side. This wall opens to the wood-floored engawa, where Western-style chairs and a table are placed.

6. In the anteroom, the closet is closed by *fusuma* the width of a tatami mat (three feet). This is the left side.

7. Right-hand side of the closet. Notice the design on the lower part of the *fusuma* and the square handhold inset.

When the *fusuma* is pushed to the right, you see hinged door and two drawers. This is the wardrobe side.

When the *fusuma* is pushed to the left, you see open shelves for bedding (*futon*).

The wardrobe contains a clothespole, a sliding shelf, and drawers for small items.

8. Opposite the closet is a Japanese clotheshanger, with hooks and bars for clothes. Below are kimonos folded in a box.

1. Here the wall is closed, as it usually is at nighttime and in winter. The translucent shoji admit light.

These shoji have nine divisions vertically. Here the lower third of each shoji is slid upward.

You can open the wall in different ways

These photographs take you into a six-tatami room in another Japanese inn, Seigaso in Kobe. The walls in this room are paper shoji plus sliding glass. The shoji open both vertically and horizontally. The glass slides horizontally. Each wall opens to a different garden view. The pattern you see below the shoji is wallpaper. In the large picture at the right, you can see across the garden to another wing of the inn. The outdoor blinds are fully let down in front of the shoji on the room opposite.

Two shoji are slid completely away, revealing a view of the garden through sliding windows, half of them clear and half frosted.

With the glass windows pushed back, you can see the garden beyond the rail of the engawa, outside the wall.

2. Here is a different garden view, from the adjacent wall. Note the roll-down bamboo blinds used to cut the glare.

3. The table is three feet square, the size of half a tatami mat. Beyond is the tokonoma wall with a scroll and a flower arrangement.

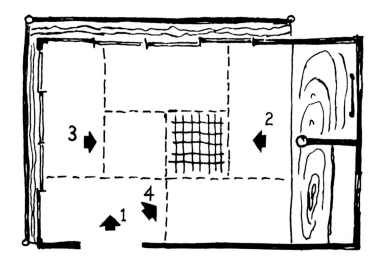

4. You sit on a cushion on the floor, with a wooden armrest (kyosoku) beside you. Notice the wood flooring of the tokonoma beyond the tatami.

In the center of the room, a table over a floor recess

Here you see one way the Japanese achieve comfort in winter. The floor recess under the table can accommodate a charcoal-fired hibachi or sometimes an electric heater (note the electric outlet in the picture on opposite page).

You sit at this table with your feet in the floor recess. Cooking may take place right at the table, sometimes over an electric hot plate.

The table can be removed and a half-tatami slipped into place here, changing the room back to a conventional all-tatami floor.

1. Once you are through the main gate, you find yourself in this entry garden. Each year new bamboos are selected and old ones removed, to keep the spatial effect as unchanging as possible.

2. The stone entry path leads you to the guest gate (with doorbell at the right); two stepping-stones lead sideways to the family entrance (which has the entry light and mailbox).

A walk through a Japanese house

The character of a Japanese house establishes itself in the entry garden. Here, in the home of Mr. and Mrs. Takeo Manabe, your first impression is one of pleasant anticipation, aroused by the garden, the gate, the fencing, and the entry path. The entry to this house is somewhat more elaborate than most, in that there are separate doors for the family and for guests. The house was designed by Isoya Yoshida and the garden by Eiijiro Nunokawa. (The garden was pictured in my book, *The Art of the Japanese Garden*.) Take a look here at what lies beyond the gate.

3. Beyond the guest gate, you come to a porch outside the guest entry to the house. Note the bench
for the comfort of waiting callers, and the sliding
door to the house. Stepping-stones (left) lead to the
rear garden.

4. (Right) The sliding front door leads to a tile-paved
genkan with polished shikidai for removing shoes.
Beyond is an interesting vista through the house to
the garden.

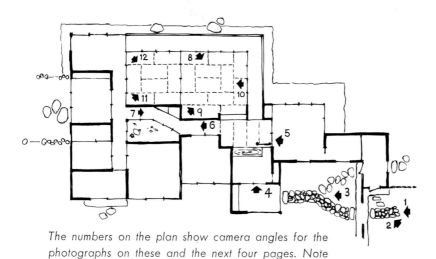

The numbers on the plan show camera angles for the
photographs on these and the next four pages. Note
the progression of garden space, including the interior
garden, as you walk through the house.

Through a
Japanese house:
Past an
interior garden

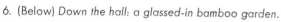
6. (Below) *Down the hall: a glassed-in bamboo garden.*

5. *Opposite the shikidai: display shelves and a translucent panel.*

7. *Opposite the bamboo garden, a display niche.*

8. On the other side of the translucent panel in the shikidai area is an alcove next to the tokonoma.

Like many present-day Japanese houses, this one has both Japanese and Western-style rooms. The view of the corridor and main room of the Manabe house shows the Japanese spirit holding up under westernization: The hallway takes a turn and leaves room for a tiny garden planted in bamboo and a niche for the display of a pottery piece. Bamboo symbolizes straightness and honesty.

Note the use of the translucent panel between the shikidai area and the main Japanese room, to carry light through the interior of the house. Note also the round peeled poles that are part of the framework of the house.

9. Translucent shoji are spacious in effect when closed; when open in any of their many combinations (see also page 63), their effect can be astonishing.

Through a Japanese house:
Achieving airy space

The Manabe house is a large house, and so it effectively demonstrates the ability of the Japanese style to manipulate space dramatically and pleasingly. The zashiki here is a ten-mat room; the adjoining room is an eight-mat room. Separately or thrown together, they seem spacious indeed.

This is also a modern house, despite the traditional appearance of its Japanese rooms. Note how, with modern technology, the architect was able to exploit glass to accentuate the effect the Japanese have always striven for. The sliding glass panels allow a horizontal opening to the garden even in cool weather, and the ceiling light fixture has the effect of a skylight.

10. With the fusuma closed this room is separated from the next one, but notice the open space above, which carries the spatial effect of the ceiling plane on beyond the temporary wall line.

With the fusuma slid back and the lower panels of the shoji open, the room gains great depth in two directions. Engawa and garden are to the right, beyond sliding glass panels that afford weather protection without shutting out the view.

11. A traditional tansu or chest provides wardrobe space and storage drawers; it is made in sections for portability (note handholds).

12. This cabinet is a bunko, made to hold stationery and writing equipment. The staggered shelf arrangement is similar to that of a chigai-dana.

Kuniyoshi Wakayama built this house in 1957. The photographs were made in 1961 when the house was just four years old. The architect was Kodo Matsubara.

This house mixes the past with the present. As the plan shows, it has both modern rooms and tatami rooms, both sliding fusuma walls and fixed Western-style walls.

The floor plan also shows the many storage wall-units the house has, each the size of one tatami. Notice, however, that the main hallway running the length of the house does not have tatami. The large room at bottom right on the plan is an office room.

Here is a modern Japanese house

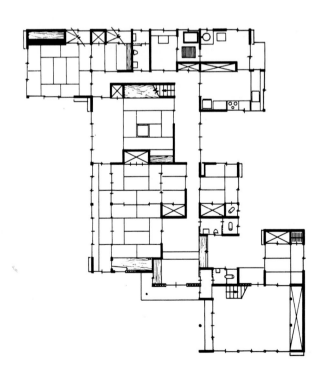

The front doors at right slide to open. The house is stucco with a concrete foundation, stone facing, and tile roof.

Here is another getabako. There are sliding doors below, sliding panels of frosted glass above. The Mondrian-like division of the glass is not at all typical of Japanese practice, but notice the traditional rounded poles set into the wall.

Entrance hall: You remove your shoes here and put on slippers. These you wear in all modern rooms with hard floors. You slip them off when you enter any tatami room. Note the getabako at the right, with small shoji above and a flower arrangement. The floor in this entry is polished pebble concrete.

This is the Western side of the room, complete with table and chairs. Note the double fusuma behind the chair (see arrow 1 on Floor Plan, page 62).

In the picture at left, the right-hand section of the fusuma has been pushed to the left. Although it opens to a hall that leads to a Japanese room, when it is closed its fusuma-like design suggests, to a Japanese, an opening to a garden.

And this is the Japanese, or tatami, side. It is winter, so a blanket is used to conserve the charcoal heat below the table. Cabinet and storage shelves can be seen in the wall under the stairway.

Japanese and Western ideas come together in a single room

In today's Japanese houses, Japanese and Western ideas sometimes share the same interior space. In this case, one end of the room has a wood floor and Western-style furniture; the other has a tatami floor and is outfitted in Japanese style.

This room also shows a typical use for storage of the space under a staircase; part is open shelves, part shelves closed off by sliding panels. Note the television and clock, teacups and trophies.

Also noteworthy is the shoji pattern on the fusuma at the left, which suggests outdoor space beyond, rather than just another interior space. To see where it leads, note the Floor Plan on page 62.

With the shoji closed, the only decorative thing you can see is the framed calligraphy high on the wall.

In a Japanese room you can select your garden view

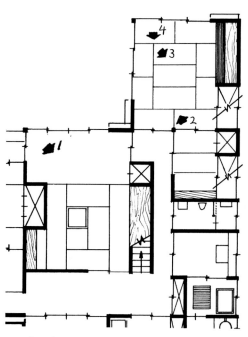

On the floor plan above, the numbers show the camera angles of the pictures here and on the next pages.

With the shoji half-open, you see a garden composition framed like a work of art (see arrow 2 on Floor Plan).

Over the centuries, the aesthetic use of the shoji wall in the home has become a hallmark of Japanese architecture. Literally, the shoji wall is manipulated. What it conceals and reveals, with its different openings, is planned and designed with utmost care.

In the picture above, your eye is drawn downward to the water garden. You can see no treetops, no sky. What you are directed to see is water spilling from the bamboo pipe, the pool catching it, and the bridge over the pool enticing you onward.

This picture, as much as any in the book, explains why the art of the Japanese house is also the art of the Japanese garden.

3. *Here you see the wife's vanity in front of a sliding fusuma (she sits on the tatami). Behind this fusuma and the one at the left go clothing and also bedding.*

How the fusuma partitions work in a bedroom-dressing room

The sliding fusuma are the secret of the economical use of interior space in Japanese houses, and also of their deceptive sense of spaciousness.

The checkerboard pattern of the fusuma you see here may seem very contemporary. Actually, it is known as the *katsura* design and goes back to the early seventeenth century.

The framed picture above the fusuma is the couple's wedding portrait. On the floor at the left is a radio. Appearing in photographs on these pages is a doll in a glass case.

4. *The fusuma opens at the left to reveal a long hallway, which runs the length of the house.*

The same fusuma opens at the right to reveal a short hallway leading to a family-style larger room (see page 61).

The fusuma above, closed, are the bedroom wall. With no furniture in view, the room seems larger than it is. These fusuma are tatami-size.

Exterior wall: The closed shoji shed a pleasingly diffused light throughout the six-mat room. At right, what look like specially decorated fusuma are really folding doors (shown also in the pictures on the facing page).

Just three rooms, but what a variety of space

The following four pages show three rooms in the Wakayama house: an eight-mat zashiki, a six-mat adjoining room containing the family shrine, and a three-mat anteroom. All nine photographs were taken from inside the zashiki. I know of no better way to demonstrate how the Japanese house uses the simplest of methods to achieve an astonishing variety and even complexity of spatial experience. Though the principal means are simple surfaces and sliding panels (fusuma and shoji), here in addition we find an unusual set of bifold doors, which also conserve usable space.

1. Exterior wall (same view as above): The open shoji reveal a wood-floored engawa with goza mat, sliding glass panels, curtains (something new in Japan), and the garden beyond. The end of the engawa is closed off by shoji.

2. The folding doors seen in the photograph at the far left are open here to reveal the butsudan, or family Buddhist shrine, set in a special alcove.

With the folding doors of the shrine open, you can see its ornate interior. Note the raised floor of the shrine alcove.

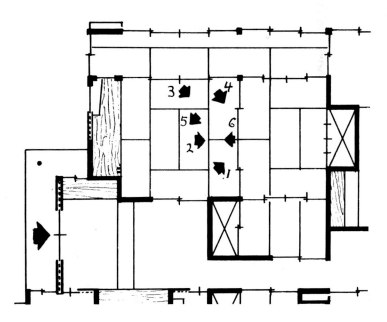

The floor plan shows the position of the camera for each numbered photograph.

3. This is the side of the room opposite from the engawa shown on page 66. The shrine doors are closed, as are the fusuma (each pair is 1½ mats wide). A gaku (painting and inscription) hangs in the open space above the fusuma.

When the fusuma are open, they extend the space of the six-mat room by three mats, or about 54 square feet. This small room serves as an anteroom from the hallway beyond; it contains a closet of one-mat dimension (see plan, preceding page).

4. Fusuma close off the zashiki from the smaller room. Note the panels above; they can also be opened and closed. For a view of these fusuma open, see page 24. A mask adorns the wall.

5. The fusuma between the zashiki and the hallway are full tatami width; grillwork divides the pair into three parts to repeat the design of the upper part of the fusuma shown at left. A corner of the tokonoma appears at the right.

6. *The tokonoma fills one end of the zashiki, and looks richly adorned despite the simplicity of the objects displayed. Note the small translucent window behind the shelf, and the modernized version of the tokonoma post (toko-bashira). The engawa is at the right.*

Three rooms: variety out of simplicity

Continuing, from the last page, our examination of the suite of three rooms, here we see how one room is used to enlarge the space of an adjoining room. An alcove like the tokonoma can do the same thing, and in addition provide a focus of interest for the room when it is closed off from the garden.

Note also one of the subtleties of the Japanese interior. Although any one of the sliding wall panels may be simplicity itself, the interior is kept from being monotonous by variations in the width of the panels and in the design. Here are four different panel designs, including that of the shoji.

The open living-dining area is divided only by the two-way fireplace. Note the sliding translucent panels in the background.

This modern house has Western-style rooms downstairs, Japanese-style rooms upstairs

The traditional Japanese house is so well worked out for Japanese needs that the Japanese have not tried to adapt more than a few of its details to changing modes of living. Instead, they will more often build separate Western-style and Japanese-style rooms. In this house, designed by architect Kiyoshi Makino for Minoru Segawa, the two different kinds of rooms are on separate floors.

The modern living room here has roll-away glass instead of shoji, and opens onto a terrace with a traditional garden.

(At right) The carpeted stairway to the second floor has a shoji-panel window and a daylit plant box.

Japanese
rooms upstairs

Upstairs, the Japanese rooms look exceedingly un-
cluttered in comparison with the Western rooms
downstairs. This house is unusual in Japan in that it
has heating; therefore, the shoji also have accom-
panying glass panels.

*1. Looking from engawa side of the eight-tatami room, you
see the tokonoma on the left, the fusuma to the three-mat
room (entry from the hall) in the center, and the shoji to
the garden at the right.*

*3. (Below) This small garden on the second floor occupies the space of three mats (6 x 9 feet). It is open to
the sky, walled on two sides, open to rooms on two sides (this view is from the larger room). Note the
bamboo engawa in the foreground. The six-foot opening to the anteroom at the left has two glass panels,
a screen panel, and two shoji panels; all slide on tracks.*

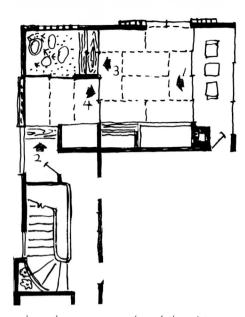

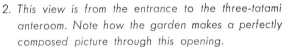

2. This view is from the entrance to the three-tatami anteroom. Note how the garden makes a perfectly composed picture through this opening.

Numbers show the camera angles of the pictures on these two pages. The stair is pictured on the preceding page.

4. From the entrance to the large room you can see the engawa on the far side. The tokonoma at the right is adorned with a scroll and a doll on a pedestal. Note the furniture on the engawa. Beyond, the sliding glass panels are more like windows, since this is a second-story room. Hanging bamboo screens provide shade from the sun. At this end of the room there is open space over the shoji, which here are not exterior wall panels.

A stone wall (with simple gates) and tall planting behind provide a double degree of privacy from the street.

Both gates open. Despite the modern treatment of the wall, the double gate is a traditional idea. Steps lead to the entry.

1. The outside entry, stone step, and hinged door are modern touches, but the execution is in the Japanese spirit.
2. The entrance hall has a wood floor; it has no kutsunugi-ishi, but does have a getabako (left). The floor is one step above the entry.

3. The tokonoma still graces the best room in the house. This somewhat modernized one retains the traditional look.

The Japanese house in transition

The lesson of this house is that the Japanese people, for all their long tradition, can be just as much individualists as anyone else when it comes to building a house.

This is the house of Sotoji Tanaka, designed by architect Hidezo Sato. The house has Japanese rooms, including a tea room, and Western rooms, including a modern kitchen. According to Japanese tradition a house cannot be separated from its garden, and so in this instance some parts of the garden are done in the Japanese manner and some in the Western, to match the rooms that open onto them. (For camera angles, see the arrow numbers on the Floor Plan, page 76.)

4. This shoji-enclosed room seems pure Japanese except for the cabinet and the picture on the wall. Note that the shadows of people in the next room can be seen on the shoji. Zabuton for seating are placed around the horigotatsu, the movable table set over a floor recess.

Japanese and Western, side by side

Here is one way to place Japanese and Western-style rooms side by side. Notice how two small rooms become one large room by the simple process of sliding away the wall that divides them.

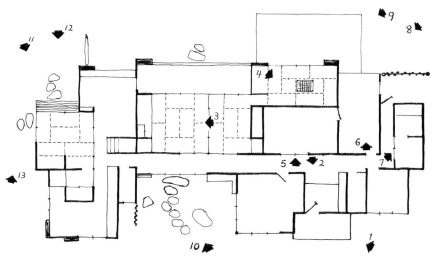

Numbers refer to camera angles for the photographs on the two preceding pages, these two pages, and the next six pages.

Slide back the shoji, and the Japanese room opens to a Western room, complete with rug on the floor, furniture, hinged door, and built-in cabinetwork. The floor and ceiling tracks mark the dividing line.

5. Seen from the Western room, the Japanese room appears spacious indeed, although it is just 7½ mats. The recess under the table can be covered by a section of tatami.

Innovations
in kitchen, bath, and laundry

Until relatively recently, short supply and great cost limited the mechanical equipment of the Japanese house, keeping it far less elaborate than that found in American homes. The Tanaka house suggests that a change is beginning to take place. Its kitchen and laundry look to the West for innovations, but in the bath new materials have simply been adapted to an old form.

6. This gleaming kitchen has a stainless steel sink and counter and all the modern appliances.

7. An innovation in the bath is the use of tile in the tub, on the wall, and on the floor. Here, the tub holds hot water; the enclosure next to it (with two boards on top), cool water for washing and rinsing. Notice the wooden drainboards set in the tile floor. An innovation in the laundry is the modern washing machine.

The garden has varied aspects

Here is the rear entry, with bathroom windows at left and kitchen windows at right (shown on the preceding page). The interesting feature is the bamboo fence with a hedge trained over it. This forms a leafy panel as seen from the garden, and a bower-like screen for the garden as seen from the rear entry.

8. Above is the end of the facade shown on the facing page. It shares a view of the Western-style section of the garden. The rear entry is behind the fence.

9. *A paved terrace with pipe-frame overhead structure (for shade from a vine or bamboo cover) is one element of the Western-style part of the garden.*

This view of the Tanaka house is taken from the part of the garden done in the Western style. The stone-paved terrace opens off the combination Western and Japanese room shown on page 77. Next on the right is a 24-foot corridor, then the children's room. Beyond the sodegaki is a tea room.

Beside each section of sliding door- and window-panels, you will notice a kind of box. This is used to store the wooden panels that are drawn over all openings (except windows that have fixed grilles) at night. They are removed each morning.

10. *Side entrance to the hallway. The setting is built around the large maple tree, several carefully placed rocks, and a stepping-stone pathway leading to the kutsunugi-ishi. Note the sodegaki at the left.*

Japanese-style garden, and a tea room

The gardens shown here belong to the house shown on the preceding eight pages, but they are as different as the Japanese- and Western-style rooms inside the house.

A tea room is built at one corner of the house. In designing it, the architect was careful to give it only a few modern details, since the tea room or tea house is as ancient and revered a form as the tea ceremony itself.

11. A corner of tea room, which is almost entirely traditional in structure. The front entrance is at left, side entrance (with *kutsunugi-ishi*) at right.

12. Family or everyday entrance to the tea room has full-height glass and shoji panels above the engawa. Stepping-stones continue around the corner at right to the side entrance.

13. The formal or side entrance to the tea room is the main entrance and is called nijiriguchi. Note the low wooden door; all who enter must stoop (and thus acknowledge humility). A bamboo window grille is above. The entire area under the wide roof-overhang is paved in exposed-aggregate concrete; beyond, the garden surface is gravel. In the background, the garden achieves depth by means of high trees planted behind lower-growing plant material.

The tsuitate is a portable single-panel screen. It is placed at the entrance to a room so that those arriving do not see directly in—thus giving the room a measure of privacy. It is also used to screen the assembly of dishes brought from the kitchen, before they are served at a dining table.

Japanese screens have many uses

Since the essence of the Japanese interior is movable and flexible space, it is only natural that such movable elements as screens should form an integral part of Japanese rooms. Here you see the two general types, *tsuitate* and *byobu,* plus an example of a similar use of screening in a Japanese garden.

A byobu is a folding screen. This one is placed in a corner for decorative purposes; screens are often objects of great artistic merit. They are also used for privacy or to stop a draft. A small one may be placed at the head of your futon when you sleep; a large six-panel screen can subdivide a room.

The screen idea outdoors: This hedge performs the same function for the entrance to the house as the tsuitate does for the entrance to a room. And like the tsuitate, it is designed to be seen from both sides. Besides its visual merits, when it is used in conjunction with a pathway it directs foot traffic along a specific route.

1. *In a large entry court of a traditional restaurant in Kyoto, with room for cars to enter and turn around, this island garden of rock, trees, lantern, and fence screens the entry from being viewed from the street.*

An island garden screens this entry

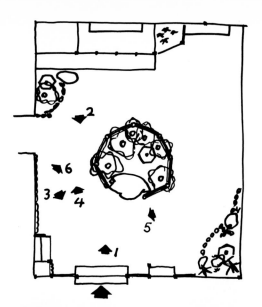

A ground plan of the entry court. The numbers are those of camera angles for the photos here and on next two pages.

2. Looking back toward the street, you see the wider of two gates, through which cars enter. The island is slightly off-center.

Your first experience with the Japanese art of screening is likely to occur as you approach a building. Here, in the entry courtyard of Isecho in Kyoto, your approach is indirect. As you pass the main gate, you know the entry must be behind the small garden, but you have to go around it to be sure—and the circular form invites you to go around. Thus, even before you are inside the building, you find you have participated in an esthetic experience.

3. *The tile-roofed traditional gate has small and large openings with sliding wooden panels.*

Isecho:
The gate and the entry

A look about the entrance court of Isecho gives you a good summary of the way the Japanese use exterior space as a prelude to the inside of the house. Notice how the garden and the structure reconcile a variety of decorative elements without seeming in the least cluttered.

4. In the corner beside the entry, a garden achieves harmony despite many varied materials: bamboo, stucco, wood siding, wood grilles. Sodegaki, lantern, tree, and stone repeat the central garden elements.

5. (Above) At the side is a roofed waiting-bench with a concrete floor. Notice the decorative bamboo wall.

6. (Below) The main entrance has sliding grille panels. To the right is another entrance.

1. *Here is how the tsuitate is most often used. Placed between two rooms (with the fusuma open), it is an effective space-divider. The mandarin duck, or oshidori, is a favorite decorative subject.*

Tsuitate: The single-panel screen

In this pair of rooms inside Isecho, you see demonstrated one of the principal uses of the tsuitate. Notice how it creates privacy and space division even though it occupies so little space itself, being merely a single panel with a frame all around. The tsuitate is usually decorated with different motifs on each side, and thus it provides a double opportunity for bringing color and design into a room.

3. *(Right) Looking in the opposite direction, you see the other side of the same tsuitate, decorated with a different painting. Note the byobu of different heights in the corners, and the gaku above.*

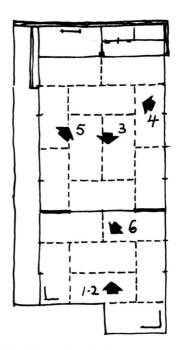

2. When the tsuitate is removed, the privacy and mystery are gone. Here you can see to the far end of the room, where the tokonoma and chigai-dana are located.

The floor plan of these two rooms; numbers show the camera angles here and on the next two pages.

By now you have seen enough tokonoma to realize that although there are basic rules, the variations are infinite. No two in Japan are alike.

The spacing varies, the wood treatment varies. Some have cabinets, some have windows; others do not. In some the floor is raised, in others it is not. A chigai-dana may accompany the tokonoma, or it may merge with it, or it may be left out. As we have seen elsewhere, within their broad tradition the Japanese are individualists in the way they build their houses.

5. (Above) *This chigai-dana adjoins the tokonoma shown on the facing page (note the post they share and the opening between them). The low cabinet has sliding doors covered with the same design as those next to the tokonoma. Here the flower arrangement, for variety, is a hanging one.*

4. (Left) *One end of the pair of rooms shown on the two preceding pages is occupied by the tokonoma. Notice the refinements in this one: the decorative edging on its tatami, the low cabinet doors, and the particularly fine design of the translucent window that lights it.*

6. (Right) *When not in actual use, byobu are usually placed in a corner, like this. The pictures on them are often seasonal. The side turned toward the room may relate to the season, but in winter the Japanese like to display a summer scene, and in summer a winter scene. The idea is to suggest warmth in winter, coolness in summer. This medium-height screen shows winter and spring subjects on its panels.*

Thus we see the thousands of possible variations in the Japanese house. It is also apparent that many Japanese ideas are adaptable to American homes—sliding wall and cabinet panels, the engawa, and perhaps even the tokonoma as a central place to display art. But at the same time one must be wary of falling under the romantic spell of the Japanese mode and copying it blindly. After all, Americans are not Japanese and they do not live the way the Japanese do, and so a Japanese house in its entirety would rarely be appropriate for an American family in America.

Part of the end of the same room shown in the picture at the left, but the fusuma are now closed. Here you see the closed storage spaces in the chigai-dana. Notice that the flower arrangement is placed on a small pedestal.

Although this tokonoma resembles the one on page 92, it is somewhat different. Notice the recessed light coming down from above. The view is from the adjoining room, through the open fusuma.

94   The same view as in the picture at the right above, but the fusuma are open now, revealing the adjoining room with its smaller tokonoma and the dining table.

Isecho: The tokonoma is sized to the room

These pages picture a large room with a large tokonoma and a chigai-dana. Adjoining it is a smaller room with a smaller tokonoma (and a closet in place of a chigai-dana). The larger room has eight mats, the smaller room six. Note how the fusuma design, the same in each room, unifies the two when the partitions are open.

The adjoining room has a table, ashtrays, two zabuton for sitting, and a hibachi for warmth.

The room is basically eight mats in size, with a ninth mat in an alcove that takes the place of a chigai-dana. The tokonoma, one mat in size, does not count in computing the size of a room. A ceramic hibachi sits beside the table.

A nine-mat room
with a low folding screen

The third room of a group of three that are interconnected is shown here. It adjoins the eight-mat room shown on page 94, and when the fusuma are removed an open space seventeen mats in size is created. Departing from the usual rule that rooms of this size have an even number of mats, this one omits the cabinets from the chigai-dana recess and covers the recess floor with a tatami, thus making an over-all floor area of nine mats.

Note this third tokonoma. It is quite different from those in the neighboring rooms.

Here is a low byobu, seen also in the right background of the photograph at the left. This screen can be used to keep a draft off the diners seated on the floor.

1. Entrance. The door with a knob (center) is the side door of the house; the tea house entry is to its right. Notice the short fence, in a style still used in (and appropriate for) front-gate areas today.

A special house for the tea ceremony

The tea house of Yoshio Ooi, in Tokyo, is over forty years old. It was well designed and built, for it survived the great earthquake of 1923. Although it has some modern touches, it also has the elements dictated by the long tradition of the tea house and the tea ceremony. And time has brought it another characteristic prized in a tea house: the mellowing that comes with age.

Here you see one of the traditional elements: a special kind of entry. On the next two pages are the side gate, side entrance through a garden, and a waiting area. And on the following four pages you get a more detailed look at what is inside.

This is a separate house devoted to the tea ceremony. For a look at a tea room that is part of the main house, turn back to page 83.

2. From the roofed entry gate, a path leads to the main entrance of the tea house. In the lower right is the beginning of the path to the side entrance; notice the large decorative rock between the two paths.

3. (Right) From inside the shikidai area (at the main entry to the tea house), looking back. Note the hinged door, unusual in Japan, and the Japanese light fixture.

4. (Right) The entrance is six feet (one mat) in width. Notice the kutsunugi-ishi set in ripple-pattern concrete (concrete has roof tile embedded in it), and the bamboo facing under the shikidai.

The traditional tea-house entry

Like the Japanese family house, the tea house also has an outdoor entry area separated from the main garden by fence or hedge, although the main garden usually can be entered from a side gate like the one shown here.

Notice the detailing of the bamboo fence, neatly and artistically tied together. The top part of each bamboo section was cut just above a joint, so that the membrane would prevent rainwater from entering and causing the bamboo to deteriorate. This style of fence is being built today in Japan; its design seems quite timeless.

5. Side gate closed. The waiting area is outside the picture, to the right.

Side gate open. Note the stepping-stone path to the side entrance.

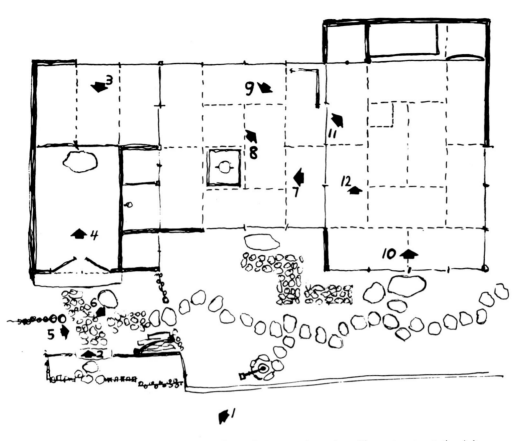

Floor and ground plan shows layout of tea house and garden. The entry is at the left. Numbers show the camera angles of photos on pages 98 to 105.

6. (Below) Here is the outside bench where guests wait until the host invites them in—traditional with a large tea house.

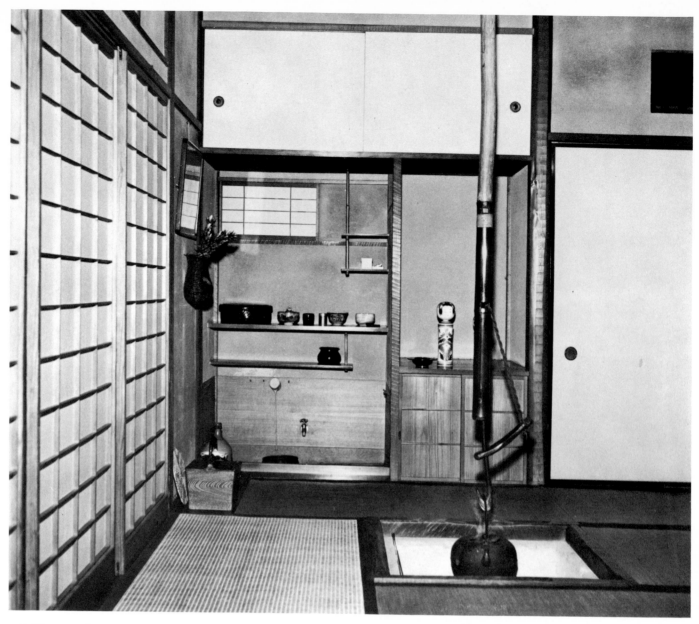

7. The paraphernalia of the tea ceremony are kept in one corner of this room, called a mizuya. It contains a sink at floor level (notice the water faucet), and cabinets and shelves for the dishes used. The teakettle is hung from the ceiling over a depression in the floor called the ro, where a charcoal fire is kindled (charcoal is smokeless) to heat the water.

8. This byobu is placed in a corner of the room shown in the photograph above; the fusuma to the main tea-ceremony room are at the right.

9. *Another view of the ro. It occupies the space of half a tatami. The shoji opens to the garden, where there is a water basin for pre-ceremony handwashing.*

A place for brewing tea

The storage place for the tea-ceremony utensils resembles a tokonoma in design (note the hand-hewn post). The shelves above the sink are suspended somewhat in the fashion of those in a chigai-dana, and the sliding cabinet doors overhead match the fusuma at the right.

10. The tokonoma in the main tea-ceremony room is the oldest shown in this book. It has an unusual old panel at the right, made of a single solid board with a carved pumpkin design; this is one of the prized parts of the tea house.

A touch of old Japan

From the adjoining room, the food and drink of the tea ceremony are brought into this one. The host and the guests are pleased to perform the ceremony in an old room, for it somehow enhances the detached atmosphere that the cult of tea deliberately seeks. As the preceding photographs in this book show, the Japanese house has changed very little in its purely Japanese aspects since the old house pictured here was built.

11. This view discloses the depth of the tokonoma, with the carved board at the right. Note the shelf behind it.

This closeup of the upper cabinet doors shows the ingenious iron door-catch, an old design but modern-looking. Note the fine woodwork.

12. To the left of the tokonoma is a built-in cabinet area. The upper cabinet has hinged wooden doors; the lower, fabric-covered sliding doors.

Closeup of the doorpull on the lower doors, showing carefully wrought iron bracket and leather pull.

(Right) The cabinet with its upper doors open, revealing a treasury of old sculpture inside.

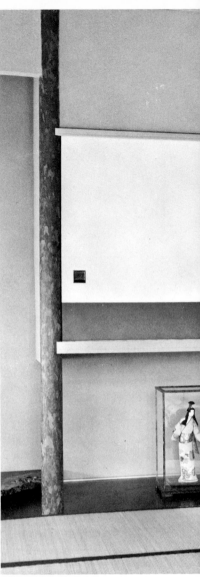

Here the tokonoma has a minimum of structure. The toko-bashira (post) divides the end wall into the traditional tokonoma and chigai-dana (the alcove-cabinet at right).

A room for the tea ceremony, modern and simple

The low entrance is called the nijiriguchi. It forces guests to stoop low to enter. A bamboo fence and a low planting can be seen through the open door.

In contrast to the tea house shown on the preceding pages, this tea room, the Yoshida-tei, is recently built and is quite simple in design. Nonetheless, it retains the traditional touches—cabinets for storing the art objects to be admired during the tea ceremony, alcoves and shelves for the discreet display of a few of these objects (here a calligraphy scroll, a flower arrangement on a log slab, and three dolls), a low entrance, and a general sense of sanctuary from the outside world. Ideally, the tea room is as simple, austere, and detached as a room in a Zen monastery, where the tea ceremony originated.

The entry door is next to the doormat. Note the stones, the lantern, and the low-growing plants that make up a miniature Japanese garden.

(Right) From the street, steps lead up to the entrance at the side of the house (as in many Japanese entries). The pattern of the shoji inside the glass windows repeats the pattern of the house siding.

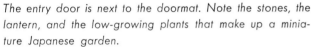

With the shoji closed, the living room has complete privacy and good diffused light.

American adaptations:
Using shoji panels over windows

The final section of this book presents American houses that use Japanese ideas to good advantage. All the houses are in the San Francisco Bay area, where Japanese influence has traditionally been strong.

The house shown on these pages belongs to my friend Fred Tsujimoto, who bought it a few years ago and has changed it to his liking. Note his use of shoji panels inside the glass windows. Turn the page to see more about them as a room divider.

Here is the living room with the shoji open in the background. The shoji in the foreground that serve as a room divider are only partly open.

A beautiful old four-panel byobu is mounted on one wall of the living room.

Shoji with an interesting pattern are used like fusuma in this room. Note the Japanese kama (used in the tea ceremony) on the table.

By moving a shoji panel, the living room (in the foreground) can be opened to the kitchen-dining room.

American adaptations: Shoji as room dividers

Even when the translucent shoji are closed, they let in light from the living room to the kitchen.

Merely sliding the shoji conceals the kitchen from the living room and reveals the passage along the side of the dining area.

Mr. Tsujimoto achieved a flexible use of space by means of sliding panels that divide a large room into two rooms that can be opened into one. Because the kitchen-dining area is windowless (lit only by a skylight and artificial lighting), he used translucent shoji instead of solid fusuma, which would have kept out light when drawn across the opening. These shoji are specially made, since the standard shoji (6 feet high) would have been too low.

The byobu is one of the finest creations of Japanese art. The handsome six-panel byobu in this photograph fills the wall above the sofa.

Just a few Japanese touches indoors, and a garden outdoors

Many Japanese materials—screens, block prints, shoji, garden ornaments, to name a few—are appropriate for American houses. But because of our way of living, it is not a good idea to attempt to use all of them as the Japanese use them. We sit on chairs, sleep in beds, and wear our shoes inside, and so it is seldom practical to reproduce a Japanese tatami room for Western-style living. Even the Japanese build Western-style rooms for these purposes, as we have seen.

Space-saving shoji are used also in the dressing-room closet.

A hall linen closet has sliding shoji panels for doors.

Like a Japanese room, this bedroom has a garden outside its glass wall—but with curtains instead of shoji to close off the view.

The garden creates
the view from indoors

The garden of the Claude Teem house was re-modeled by the author. In it, I tried to show that the Japanese effect can be achieved with a combination of Japanese and American materials. The stone lanterns, the water basin, and the dried bamboo used on the fence came from Japan. All the other materials, stones, and plants are from local sources (it is a good idea to use plant material from your own locality, to be sure it will be adapted to your climate). The total effect is created not by the materials themselves but by how you use them.

The feeling of a Japanese garden can be created by using similar ideas but materials that are at hand. The materials employed in this little garden are pebbles, soy tubs, and bamboo (on the wall and atop the concrete retaining wall). The garden is outside the breakfast-room window.

(At left) The view from every window has been thoughtfully composed. Here, seen from third-floor stair, is a zigzag garden stairway with low plants on each side. Notice that the seams in the fence at the right are covered by half-stalks of bamboo.

This view of the garden atop the steep slope gives you an idea of its small size, although it looks large from inside the house. Compare this view with the picture on page 113.

On the upper level is a pond surrounded by a bridge, stone lanterns, rocks, and American-grown plant materials. The bridge was designed and built in America, but the effect is Oriental.

Adaptations inside the house

A kakeziku (scroll) makes a fine decoration for any vertical wall space. The one shown above is in a hallway of the home of Karl Rhode-Hamel, A.I.D.

The kakeziku over the tansu was selected in Japan by Karl Rhode-Hamel for his own home. The ceramic fruit and cup were made by his wife Irene.

In Japan a gaku, or framed brush painting, is often hung on the wall over the fusuma or shoji. This one is the center of interest of a built-in buffet in an American home. Observe how its lines take on an almost tokonoma-like appearance when a flower arrangement, a Japanese wooden rice container, and a ceramic ashtray set are appropriately placed on top of the buffet.

In their living room, the Rhode-Hamels have created a feeling of Japanese living by using a large screen on the wall, zabuton on the sofa, and a low table and chairs. (See also page 124.)

Adaptations
in the garden

A portable fence, shown also in the picture at right, below. You can glimpse the garden beyond the fence, which is merely tied together with twine.

In the rear garden at the home of John Pollia. The garden was designed by the author. The portable fence is one of many Japanese touches: a bamboo sodegaki, live bamboo for harmony, and stepping-stones that lead around the sodegaki to the stairs.

and on the street

Sodegaki on a city street. This neat and simple fence-shield was designed by owner Sam Jermane. It is on the side facing his neighbor's house. Note how the bark bamboo trim continues up the corner of the house.

(Below) The opposite side of the sodegaki creates the impression of a private, individual entry garden. Note the stone lantern and the collection of plants in containers.

Two kakeziku make a stunning group on the dining-room wall. You can get a vertical effect from one or two, or a horizontal effect from two or more, depending on the way you group them.

Decorating with screen, scroll, tansu, and bonsai

You can tell by looking around the Robert C. Bergins' house that they like Japanese objects of art and understand how to use them to enhance their home. You might suspect also that they are interested in bonsai, the art of miniature trees—and you would be right. They have made hundreds of them, some of which they display inside the house, others in the garden. For more on their house, turn to the next page.

When they remodeled, the Bergins added this alcove especially for a tansu. It can be seen from the entry as well as here, from the bedroom. Note the overhead lighting, the bonsai, and the goza mat on the floor.

One wall of the living room shows a handsome four-panel screen over the writing desk. The byobu blends well with almost any style of furniture, but of course the relationship between the elements determines the effect. Note the maple bonsai on the desk.

Here are two units of a tansu placed side by side (also shown in the picture at the right). A scroll, framed Japanese wood-block prints, and two bonsai complete the composition.

More ways Americans use the tansu

Even though, in Japan, tansu are seldom displayed in the main part of the house, in America they are considered handsome pieces of furniture. They are compatible with many furniture styles. In Japan, their primary use is for storing clothes and personal belongings, but here they are used successfully wherever a storage chest or table may be needed. The Bergins have them in the dining room and hall as well as in the bedroom.

From the hall, looking toward the glass door in the bedroom of the Bergins' house is like looking at a picture. Beyond the door is an engawa, with a platform for bonsai, a Buddha figure, and a wooden lattice grille, used as the Japanese would use such a screen.

A single tansu in the dining room. Its horizontal line is balanced by tall candlesticks and the tall podocarpus in the container.

Looking through the glass wall into the garden. Above it is a gaku, as in Japan. The chief difference is the sliding glass windows and bamboo shades instead of shoji.

In America, the fun of a Japanese room

The adjoining bedroom looks through retracted shoji toward the tokonoma in a Japanese room. The fusuma at the right are closet doors.

Many American families who visit Japan come home charmed by the experience and, more than that, with the wish to re-create a bit of Japan in their own homes.

These pictures show the accomplishments of one such family. The Karl Rhode-Hamels, after several trips to Japan, proceeded to build a Japanese addition to their house, and also to make a Japanese garden.

What they achieved is handsome, workable, and a delight to their friends. It seems to me also a proper and promising closing to this book on the Japanese house, which after all is written for Americans.

Japanese Rooms in America

This photograph shows the relationship of the bedroom to the Japanese room. The floor of the Japanese room is raised several inches, and both it and the bedroom floor are covered with goza mats.

Here the shoji are partially closed for privacy. Since the floors are goza rather than tatami, shoes can be worn in these rooms, although you would not do so in Japan.

The Japanese room adjoining the bedroom features a low table and zabuton for seating. Beyond is the garden.

GLOSSARY

bonsai—miniature tree-landscapes, dwarfed by special methods of culture

bunko—book case, book cabinet, or storage cabinet for writing materials

butsudan—family Buddhist shrine

byobu—a multiple-panel folding screen

chigai-dana—a pair of shelves in a side alcove used for display

daidokoro—kitchen

engawa—narrow wooden platform at the wall line, between the shoji and the rain shutters; it is a veranda, a porch, a stoop, an open corridor, a balcony (the engawa can be any or all of these)

furo—bath

fusuma—sliding interior wall panels

futon—bedding

gaku—framed calligraphy panel or brush painting

genkan—entry vestibule

geta—Japanese outdoor footwear

getabako—cabinet for storing shoes, geta, slippers, umbrellas

goza—a mat, a floor covering (material is same as the surface of the thick tatama mat)

hibachi—Japanese charcoal brazier

horigotatsu—floor recess usually one-half tatami in size; a charcoal or electric heater goes in the recess, with table above and quilt over the table

kakeziku—a hanging scroll

kama—kettle

kamoi—a lintel with shallow grooves on the under side that serve as tracks for fusuma

kutsunugi-ishi—taking-off-shoes stone

kyosoku—wooden armrest

mizuya—a washing place in the tea-ceremony room; also a cupboard for tea equipment

monoire—a closet; a storage room

nijiriguchi—the side or formal entrance to the tea room

oshidori—mandarin duck; a favorite decorative subject

ro—a hearth; a depression in the floor of the tea ceremony room for a charcoal fire

shikidai—intermediate step or platform between the kutsunugi-ishi (taking-off-shoes stone) and the house floor

shogi—Japanese chess

shoji—paper-covered sliding wall panels

sodegaki—a short screening fence

tabi—Japanese socks with a separate part for the big toe

tansu—a chest of drawers; a cabinet; a bureau

tatami—straw mats (usually 3 by 6 feet and a little over 2 inches thick) used for floor surface in the Japanese house

toko-bashira—a specially crafted alcove post placed between the tokonoma and the chigai-dana area, usually near the center

tokonoma—an alcove in the principal Japanese room (zashiki) where art treasures, natural objects, and/or flower arrangements are displayed

tsuitate—a portable, single-panel screen

yokushitsu—bathroom

zabuton—cushions used as seats

zashiki—principal room in a Japanese house; a kind of all-purpose room

zori—straw sandals; Japanese slippers with flat bottoms